ALL THE PAINTINGS OF
BOTTICELLI

Part I

VOLUME TWENTY-FIVE
in the
Complete Library of World Art

The Complete Library of World Art

ALL THE PAINTINGS

OF BOTTICELLI

Part 1 (1445-1484)

By ROBERTO SALVINI

Translated from the Italian by
JOHN GRILLENZONI

HAWTHORN BOOKS, INC.
Publishers · *New York*

Printed and bound in Great Britain by
Jarrold & Sons Ltd, Norwich

CONTENTS

555

ALL THE PAINTINGS OF
BOTTICELLI

SANDRO BOTTICELLI

Life and Work

SANDRO BOTTICELLI is now among the best-known and most celebrated artists of the Italian Quattrocento. While he was living the favors of the Medici family poured on him, and with them the understanding and the applause of that rare *élite*—the artists, humanists, philosophers and poets—who gathered at the Court of the enlightened rulers of Florence. He was also chosen (with other fashionable painters) to decorate the Sistine Chapel. But after his death, there was no one capable of carrying on his art, and history soon forgot him.

In the spring of 1510 he died and left his painting at a crucial moment in the history of art—when taste in Florence was undergoing a swift and radical change. He was present, early in 1500, when Leonardo returned from Milan as the celebrated painter of *The Last Supper* and was soon to begin his *St Anne* and the *Mona Lisa*. Leonardo da Vinci and Michelangelo were at this time preparing for the decoration of the Hall of the Great Council in the Palazzo Vecchio. With these monumental designs (Leonardo's *Battle of Anghiari* and Michelangelo's *Battle of Cascina*) Leonardo and Michelangelo became the master artists of their generation. And it was at this same time, about 1504, that Raphael arrived in Florence, anxious to learn, and to begin his splendid series of *Madonnas*. The artistic vision of each of these artists was different from the other, but none the less

9

alike in their attempt to create unity from the dynamic combination of plastic and pictorial elements. It is easy to understand, therefore, why Botticelli's painting should seem obsolete by comparison, almost a shadow of a bygone age. His art was so intimate, so typical of the Quattrocento, in the neat pattern of extremely pure plastic and linear rhythms that were woven together with the least play of movement or background. At times it was so archaic, especially the later works, both in symbolic content and in form, that the artist resorted to almost Neo-Gothic principles of composition.

Thus, despite the complete account of his work, and indeed the praise, Botticelli appears as a lesser figure in Vasari's *Lives*. We read charming anecdotes, we note the certain moralizing insistence on the "little control" which forced the artist to an impoverished and desolate old age, and the somewhat distracted praise Vasari gives to the most famous works, *The Birth of Venus* and the *Primavera*, where the Graces "... are expressed by him with grace." These are the themes in Botticelli's biography. Vasari adds only one penetrating critical note when he speaks of the *St Augustine* (plates 78–79) in the Church of Ognissanti. Here he admits giving way to the moral anxiety which is expressed by that figure and in the tension of the lines which strain to hold in the powerful, bold planes.

For centuries afterwards not only were the reasons for the artist's greatness no longer understood, but even his major works were forgotten. At the end of the eighteenth century, Abbot Lanzi, who knew much about the fortunes of Italian art, and understood (with Mengs) the rather difficult paintings by Masaccio, knew Botticelli only by the Sistine frescoes and by "many paintings of little figures, where at times he might be confused with Mantegna [*sic*], if his heads had not been more gracious."

We owe Botticelli's rediscovery to the lively and inspired English critics who came to the fore in the late nineteenth century as part of the Pre-Raphaelite movement. Ruskin was the first to interpret the moral content that lies hidden beneath the refined, formal aestheticism when he said, in a daring comparison, that Botticelli was a reformer of the Church equal to Luther. He grasped the essence of his style when he defined Botticelli's painting as a "play of pure line." Walter Pater found in Botticelli a tinge of inexpressible melancholy, a sense of exile, almost of regret for a full and active life of human beings who had been enchanted by dreaming of a contemplative life.

But as opinions about the artist spread, he became known as an ingenuous "primitive," sighing and dreaming, an image which caused some reservations among more positive historians. Cavalcaselle, for instance, could only admire the neatness of his drawing and craftsmanship of his execution, but he noted a lack of "academic" correctness in his work and the rather wild nature of his figures. Muntz preferred Ghirlandaio for his "genius as virile and robust as his rival's was delicate and effeminate." It was Berenson who found a relevant definition, in the last decade of the nineteenth century, of the artist's style. His definition is strictly formalistic, but if considered without Berenson's rather frail theoretical premises, his insight succeeds in penetrating those values of musical linearity which underlie Botticelli's idiom and which later criticism, especially Adolfo Venturi's and Yukio Yashiro's, elucidated so well. But it is necessary also to discuss Botticelli's lyric tone and that individual quality of feeling in his art. For this evaluation we turn to the critics Bettini and Lionello Venturi. But since morality is part of the artist's feeling, as well as his intelligence and his experience, the critics were faced with the problem of determining

Botticelli's relations with his milieu. A number of notable studies with broad viewpoints arose from this question; for instance, the monographs by Mesnil and by Argan. On the lines these men laid down—and bearing in mind the analytic contributions made by Ulmann, Bode, Horne and Gamba—I should like to trace briefly a "profile" of the artist.

He was born in Florence, in 1445, Alessandro di Mariano Filipepi, but soon came to be called Botticelli (or *little casks*), from his brother's nickname, Giovanni Sensale (or "John the Dealer"). His first dated work is the *Allegory of Fortitude* (plate 20) painted in 1470 for the Merchants' Guild. To arrive at this point he had to be educated first, and to serve an apprenticeship. He received a not indifferent (for those times), humanistic education and spent a few years, as Vasari tells us, in Fra Lippo Lippi's studio. It is difficult to imagine the contrasting temperaments working together. Botticelli was sensitive, saddened, while Lippi tended to be serene and imperturbable. The older painter, not insensitive but always in possession of himself, went through a number of phases, from the troubled plasticity of Masaccio (from its beginnings right through the intermediary, lyric period inspired by Fra Angelico) to the new, almost olympic classicism of his own late works. A careful analysis could profitably reveal what elements in Lippi's late style contributed to the formation of the young painter's style. Perhaps the connecting-point lies in the famous *Madonna and Child with St John the Baptist* in the Uffizi Gallery, which, according to the best sources, Lippi painted a little after 1460.

The composition recommends itself especially for the quiet plastic rhythm which creates a sense of thoughtful serenity, a sense shared by the most classic art of the Florentine Quattrocento (we might include some of the great, late creations of Luca della Robbia). But this slow and calm play of forms takes place with a new pictorial refinement in the delicate action of the light which flows across the surfaces, softening all the hardness and muting the harsh relief of the rounded volumes. The outside line blends into the light, thus joining the figure pictorially with the background. Botticelli could not have found this kind of softness or such a mellow and broad development of masses in the work of any other painter of his time. These were indispensable bases from which to proceed to an art motivated essentially by the "unfolding" of its lines. In such an art, the volume or mass, instead of floating freely in space, is related to the main plane and participates in the play among the subtly stratified planes of the picture. We can see this clearly in Lippi's *Madonna* in the disc-like aspect which the Madonna's face assumes, the single plane of her face and the Child's, as well as of her hands joined in prayer.

The relationship between the figures and the background, in which they fuse by blending the outside line with the marginal light, suggested to Botticelli a relationship between figure and landscape, between form and space, quite different from that accepted as dogmatic by the painters of the early Quattrocento. What Botticelli saw as a possible relationship did not deny the principles of perspective vision, but loosened the framework by subordinating the distant to the near objects.

The harmonious turning of the volumes in a rhythm that was related to a plane must have evoked to the eyes of the young apprentice the infinitely expressive possibilities available to the artist who could somehow translate that harmony (still purely plastic) into terms of line. Line, that is, which would unfold with equal harmony.

We have a series of *Madonnas* derived from Lippi's which

were quite early identified as Botticelli's work (plates 1, 125, 126). Here is evident the attempt to detract from the harmonious relationship of the volumes in order to find a new organizational principle by concentrating the movement of the figures in the foreground and flattening out the rounded forms of the original on a plane. The result is somewhat weak and uncertain, because the new linear thinness ends by elaborating a more sensitive kind of image without ever going beyond a merely illustrative level. But happier results are not long in appearing, as we can see in the *Madonna and Child with Angel* in Ajaccio (plate 2), where the painter becomes more independent of the original, even in his theme. There are clear signs of a new style, even if it is still incapable of informing the whole composition.

In the meantime, and—we assume—while he was still working in Fra Lippi's *bottega*, Botticelli began looking at the work of his Florentine contemporaries. Verrocchio, for example, could tell him about the expressive value of lines that suggest motion; Baldovinetti was attempting to translate into more subdued tones and more intimate accents the great unity between form and space which Piero della Francesca had realized in a section of his frescoes in Arezzo.

Instead of a neat separation of volumes within a space which would be felt as just a negative volume, Baldovinetti imagined a kind of inlaying of the figure into the background. In his fresco in the Church of the Annunziata, *The Nativity* and in his *Virgin* in the Louvre, we see that the form stops on the threshold of space, and the limiting function is exercised by the line which holds the form in suspended immobility. The stillness is animated, however, by a subtle but very perceptible vibration from within.

The most obvious signs of Botticelli's approach to Baldovinetti's vision are the cypresses in the background of a few youthful paintings of the *Madonna* or the graduated, hilly landscapes behind some youthful portraits. Apart from these details, the painting in Alessio must have stimulated the artist's desire for a vibrant outer line which would be capable of isolating the form in a rhythm closed off from the surrounding space.

An echo of Baldovinetti, and a first timid approach to Verrocchio, can be sensed in the *Madonna of the Loggia* (plate 3), while the *Guidi Madonna* (plate 4) and the *Madonna and Child* formerly in Périgueux and now in the Louvre (plate 5) reveal a desire to combine some accents of Verrocchio with Lippi's soft forms. In the *Madonna and Child with St John the Baptist* in the Accademia, Florence (plate 6), the first hints of Botticelli's own style begin to show. Note certain graceful rhythms of line, and the slow turning of the two angels around the Virgin.

We come now to the delicate *Madonna and Child with St John*, also in the Louvre, which can be understood as a version —intimate and mature—of an old theme of Lippi's. Botticelli must have painted it in an isolated and inspired moment.

The easy, cradled movement of the three images, a motif in Fra Lippo's compositions, is here transposed into a light undulation of line on a thin, formal design. Variations of this theme can be seen in the *Madonna and Child* in Washington (plate 11) and in the *Madonna and Child with Youth* in the Duveen Collection (plate 10), but here a certain weight in the form, inspired by Verrocchio, makes the rather placid turning of volumes (a characteristic taken from Lippi's *Madonna*) more thoughtful. A slow unfolding of the line takes place in a minor key, echoed by the bend in the river.

Up to this point we might say, Verrocchio's partial influence on Botticelli shows as a weighing down of Lippi's tender forms and contributes to the expression of a more meditative spirit. But for a brief time, Botticelli's study of formal solidity in Verrocchio's manner leads to a rather programmatic quality in his work. We might even suppose that after Botticelli left Lippi—who then was almost always in Spoleto—he spent some time between 1468 and 1470 in Verrocchio's workshop. The quality of the academic exercises which the painter probably experimented with during this period is identifiable even in the insistence on one or two themes, more or less the same sort of thing which characterized his first imitations of Lippi. The theme of the Virgin and three figures in an enclosure, with a garden in the background, is repeated several times (plates 12b, 13a and b). One can certainly see in these paintings the progress he made in developing greater formal beauty and restudying problems of form.

But the proved path was the one that led to Verrocchio's "school" which for other painters, like Lorenzo Credi and Botticini, had become the goal of every expressive possibility. Thus artistic intention had to impress itself on materials that were inflexible. But Botticelli's more sentimental preferences, frustrated by this hardness in Verrocchio's style, expressed themselves in the attitudes and the gestures, in the psychology of figures. But he could only manage a tone of distracted sentimentalism, and the means he used were inappropriate. We feel a greater sincerity, in this period, in what are probably his first attempts at portraiture, a genre he develops more fully later on.

We can cite, for instance, the *Portrait of a Young Man* in the Hutton Collection (plate 18), where the absorption in the face with its large eyes—with all the solidity of Baldovinetti modified somewhat by a touch of Lippi's softness—seems to extend to the clear and far landscape (reminiscent of Piero della Francesca). Perhaps nature here seems a trifle extrinsic

16

and literary. Or we can cite the portrait in the Pitti Palace (plate 19), where the boy's body turns assertively and solidly, much in the manner of the portrait by Andrea del Castagno in the Mellon Collection. But here the figure separates from the background, not only because of the chromatic contrast between the intense red of the tunic, the black of the cowl, and live blue of the sky, but also because of the incisiveness of the outline, the harshness of the folds in the drapery, the crumpled collar, the severe lining out of the face and arch of the mouth. Gone are the bemused attitudes of the early *Madonnas*; we have now insight into an interior life.

Other *Madonnas* (plates 14 and 15) are animated by a restlessness which had its origins in the painting of Antonio del Pollaiuolo. The *Allegory of Fortitude* (plate 20) of 1470 is not only the first entry in Botticelli's chronology, but also the point where Pollaiuolo's influence is grafted on to Verrocchio's. Pollaiuolo demonstrated (for the first time in the Florentine Quattrocento) how line could be used to organize and articulate the plastic form by means of an uninterrupted and unresolved tension. Only by trying out a line that would render the formal and compositional structure could Botticelli go beyond the Florentine tradition of balance, both plastic and spatial. The *Allegory of Fortitude* reveals an essential displacement of the norm. Despite the perspective perfection of the throne, the figure does not occupy space with its own mass, but emerges from the surface so as to emphasize against the horizontal plane a system of interlacing lines in a rhomboidal figure, which define the image in the very act of spiritualizing it, and give it a subtle, spiritual restlessness. The vigor of the line is very marked and animates the well-turned Verrocchian forms with a new restlessness, pointed up by the strange glints of the burnished bronze tones.

The allegory lies not only in the attributes, but rather in this detachment of the figure from time and space, in the continuous vibration that means more than any specific act. Botticelli's art at this moment, was centred on two ideals: the transfiguration of *truth* into *beauty*, and the discovery of moral meaning in beauty.

Such dense expressiveness cannot be found in the *Madonna Enthroned with Saints* (plate 22), in which we may recognize the altarpiece of the Convertite. Imagination cannot seem to find a way between the narrowness of the subject represented and the monumental theme. Some pleasant features strike the eye, however, such as St Catherine's face (plate 25), a delicate profile rendered in very clear colors and pulsing with life as the undulating lines of the hair fall under the crystalline transparency of the veil. We should observe that this was Botticelli's first attempt at narrative with the small panels in the Johnson Collection (plates 26–29) which may have formed the predella of the altarpiece. Among the barren, almost monastic architecture and backgrounds of peaceful marine blue, he disperses subtle and vibrant figurines, from which he eliminated any dramatic clarity (in one by taking away any precise relation between volume and space). They seem to exist, rather, in a gentle, fearful commotion.

The *Adoration of the Magi* in London (plates 32–33) is a highly problematic painting. The Kings' procession breaks through from the left, clamorous and agitated, along a path scooped out from beneath a high rock wall. But in the center, an architectural area of immobile columns and walls worn by time stems all the tumult. The figures range themselves solemnly in the open rectangle of space, calling to mind Lippi's firm composition in the Duomo in Prato. But in such a solid framework the figures circle restlessly because of the tense and contradictory turning of the line, much in the manner of Pollaiuolo. The somewhat encumbered composition, and the obvious influence of Lippi on many of the figures, have led most critics to date this work early in Botticelli's career. But Pollaiuolo's themes and evidence of "the vital qualities of the Botticelli line" (A. Venturi), even if oriented toward fantastic effects, make this a work painted after 1470. A close study of the panel reveals the collaboration of Filippino Lippi, whose presence in Botticelli's workshop has been documented in 1472.

Perhaps we are dealing here with a first attempt by a very young, but precocious, Lippi, assisted generously by Botticelli. Or perhaps this is a composition Botticelli had planned many years earlier, and then, around 1472, taken up again and finished with Lippi's help. It confirms Botticelli's more mature treatment of Pollaiuolo's idiom, which can be seen in several portraits (plates 36–37) done in this period, and in the lovely *Madonna of the Eucharist* (plate 35). We ought to deal with this painting separately from the group of Verrocchio-like *Virgins*, of lesser quality, with which it is ordinarily associated. The springing line definitely recalls Pollaiuolo, despite the lingering touch of Verrocchio in the symbols. The limpid landscape rests between the diverging axes of the two figures not as a superfluous decoration, but as a felt space. The energetic lines fix the images in a posture of meditation and emotional preoccupation. Now his technique becomes more precise and more capable of expressing a vision which raises to a higher pitch of contemplation the subtle, almost grieving, restlessness of the spirit. We cite here the *tondo*, *Adoration of the Magi* (plate 38), in London. Related to the London painting is the small Florentine panel of the *Discovery of the Murder of Holfernes* (plate 43), not only because of the reappearance of the vibrant Pollaiuolo line, but also because of the application in reverse of the same compositional scheme. Two groups converge from below toward the Virgin in the *Adoration of the Magi*, and the rising of the improbable architecture right to the top of the *tondo* makes the object of their aspiration seem even more distant. In the Uffizi painting, on the other hand, two groups converge in a descending movement and stop suddenly at the edge of an ideal space, made more perceptible by the steep gradation of the heads which break up the space between the drapery and the corpse. The movement begins and ends within the space enclosed by the drape, framed by the two lines which echo one another: the drape above and the body below. Thus the dramatic passing of the moment is suspended, just as if, instead of being caught at the instant when it happened, it were evoked from memory.

The artist aims even closer to the essential in the other panel of the diptych, *Judith with the Head of Holfernes* (color plate 2). The rapid movement of the maid's silhouette is caught and held by the more complex and subtle modulation of Judith's figure. Here the crescent shape of her body is balanced by the opposite curve of her right arm, prolonged by the extended scimitar, which then becomes part of the rhythm of the whole figure again through the subtle curve of the olive branch. A movement, therefore, which takes form through the well-modulated line, against the upright immobility of the tree, completes the unity of the composition. Thus the brief moment of stasis is prolonged indefinitely, outside time. The motion passes into memory. Even the frenetic little figures of the soldiers in the distant valley become projections on this screen of memory. The beauty of this small painting, even at such an early point in the development of the artist, stems from his capacity to render action and history as contemplation and myth.

The *St Sebastian* in Berlin (plate 45) seems to be the one

identified by an early source as finished in January 1474, for the Church of Santa Maria Maggiore in Florence. It represents the closest approach to Pollaiuolo's functional line. The *St Sebastian* has sometimes been criticized for the studied quality of the nude figure, as if art had been used for anatomy lessons, or criticized because the artist was too imitative of his example, which could have been Antonio and Piero Pollaiuolo's *St Sebastian* in the National Gallery, London. Vasari dates the Pollaiuolo to 1475, but Botticelli may have seen it in their workshop. Little note seems to have been taken of the fact that Botticelli has transmuted the Pollaiuolo figure by "counterleaning" the main parts of the nude in the ancient Greek manner. The straight leg plays against the bent one, the shoulder lowers corresponding to the weight-bearing leg, the head turns the opposite way. It is true that the Greek canon is emptied of its original meaning by replacing the proportional composition of the volumes with the linear articulation of the form. But the *allusion* to the ancient world projects the figure into a suggestive distance, and gives it a poetic context, just as a quoted fragment of an old poem enriches the quality of a new one. The Saint emerges from any historical relation, freed from the limitations that Pollaiuolo's archers, for instance, inflict on their version of the martyrdom, and stands alone against the receding landscape as a pure image. The dramatic torment of the Pollaiuolo martyr, expressed by a continuous, unresolved tension, here seems placated by the way Botticelli harmonized the vibrating movement of the line with the classical equilibrium of the stance.

During this period, Botticelli exploited what he had learned from the Pollaiuolo brothers in a striking series of portraits beginning with the *Portrait of a Man with a Medal* (plate 47). This has been mistakenly attributed to his workshop or to the period of the monotonous series of *Madonnas* before 1470. This dating is impossible if one studies the definite clarity of the idiom, which is a sign of a mature artist, or the incisive force of the line which recalls Pollaiuolo. The penetrating psychology of this portrait is not merely a fact of nature translated into paint, but becomes part of the artist's vision, realized with immediate facility in the vibrating texture of the lines which themselves are taken from the winding landscape.

Nor is there any reason to doubt that Botticelli did the *Portrait of a Young Woman* in the Pitti Palace (plate 51), a delicate image in which the quiet blending of the colors relates to a slow rhythmic line, again reminiscent of Pollaiuolo. This reminiscence is repeated in the same way in the *St Sebastian* in Berlin.

In the same spirit of abstraction and contemplative isolation, Botticelli painted the little-known, and frequently unaccepted, *Portrait of Lorenzo the Magnificent* (plate 48a) and the very famous *Portrait of Giuliano de' Medici* (plate 48b), probably 1475 or 1476. He did another portrait of Giuliano a few years later, after the young man's tragic death, this time in a splendid, incisive profile which seems to isolate the face in a separate world.

Poggi proved that Botticelli painted the standard with the figure of Pallas Athena, which Giuliano de' Medici carried in the tourney of 1475, but only an echo remains in the intarsia of a door in the Ducal Palace in Urbino, which was apparently copied from the Botticelli work (plate 146). From this and other intarsias in Urbino (plates 149–151) which also seem to derive from Botticelli's drawings and which date to about 1476, we can deduce the persistent influence of Pollaiuolo's tense linearity.

This is still present, but modified and loosened in a freer

composition, in the *Adoration of the Magi*, once in Santa Maria Novella but now in the Uffizi (plates 52–57), which Botticelli must have painted around 1476–77. The brilliant *mise en scène*, with its rocks and crumbling walls broken by weeds, the rotting beams and the massive timbers, the Roman ruins, the festive variety of colors in the dress of the superb collection of figures, their variegated poses, the portrait-like actuality of the heads, which we recognize as the great Medici, Cosimo the Elder and Lorenzo the Magnificent (plates 53 and 54 respectively)—all add to the great popularity of the work. The tense linear rhythm again recalls Pollaiuolo, in figures like the page at the right with Lorenzo's features (who mirrors exactly a similar figure in the scene of Zaccariah in one of the Duomo tapestries). The energy of the lines which embody the very mobile faces of the personages, are as remarkable as Botticelli's effort to stylize the restless lining of the wall joints and to render the airy thinness of the falling arcade.

The work can be compared, in its tendency toward the illustrative, to the dignified and colorful costume parades of so many contemporary compositions by artists like Ghirlandaio. But there is something more: the merely scenic unity here becomes a rigorously expressive unity. The varied movement in the lines, colors and forms of the bystanders converges slowly toward the figure of the Virgin, whose vertical rhythm is taken up again by St Joseph (plate 53). The warm vitality of that gathering passes imperceptibly to the very perceptible vibrancy of the sacred group, and as in a dream, the architecture, always thinner and more spectral, and the colors, always clearer and more transparent, pervade the image. Here again Botticelli transforms an historical fact into a detached image, a mythic memory, of a moving vision that, although subdued, is pervaded by anxiety.

The *Portrait of a Man*, formerly in the Museo Filangieri, (plate 61) which is so similar to the heads in the *Adoration*, confirms the tendency in Botticelli's style toward relaxing the linear tension he derived from Pollaiuolo. Other confirmations of this sort are the *Madonna of the Sea* (plate 62), falsely attributed to Filippino Lippi, and the *Raczinsky Madonna* (plate 63), where the touch here and there of some assistant hardly mars the beauty. We cannot ascribe Botticelli's insistent use of the circular frame for stories or groups to the fashion of the times or to the whims of his patrons. The artist was probably seeking a closed and self-contained rhythm that would best lend itself to that kind of composition. The *Raczinsky Madonna* is a case in point, because the effect derives from the coherence between the central figures and the two choral groups which are joined to the circular surface by the repeated verticals of the lilies.

We now approach the beginning of Botticelli's most brilliant period, a golden era which opens with the *Primavera* (plates 64–65) and ends with the *Birth of Venus* (Part 3, plates 12–13). During this time, the artist painted another portrait (plate 60), still austerely posed, but more detached from reality, and frequently attributed erroneously to Filippino Lippi, and drew the *Three Angels* in a lunette (plate 58) who are a prelude to the lyric rhythm of the three Graces (plate 66). The dialectical relation between the line and the form is already resolved in favor of the line, which alone generates the plastic rhythm of the images.

The *Primavera* (plates 64–77), probably painted in 1477 or 1478, not—as was long held—for Lorenzo the Magnificent, but for Lorenzo di Pierfrancesco, is an allegory of the reign of Venus, in which she is interpreted as Humanity. The allegory comes from the Neoplatonic philosophy of Marsilio Ficino, and the identification of Venus with humanity probably alludes to an ideal harmony or unity between nature and civilization. We can say that the painter, in creating a harmonious and, in its way, classic work, felt intensely this spirit of balance and unity between the freshness of living according to nature and the moral nobility of humanism. He expressively affirmed the teachings of Poliziano and Ficino, who were counselors to the young noblemen to whom the painting was dedicated. Beauty is born at the moment when natural instinct is elaborated with learning and civilization. In this painting, in fact, we see expressed the consonance between man and nature, and the Florentines of the Quattrocento could probably see in it the closest meaning of classical myth as the figures and the golden grove of orange trees uniformly unfold in the horizontal rhythm of a frieze. The trees support the visual value of the figures by opening around Venus and becoming dense behind the Graces.

Here we still have the extension of pure plastic rhythms into three-dimensional space of the Quattrocento, but the perspective has given way somewhat to another plane of reference for the arabesques of line, by the repeated divisions of the tree-trunks and the pale tint of the sky.

Line plays a freer part, as the action precipitates, in the figures of Flora and Zephyr (plate 72), then seems to spend its energies in the froth of veils around the nymph. But it renews itself by describing restless arabesques in the sinuous outlines of the body and draperies of Hora. Space interrupts the play for an instant, but the line picks up again in a slower movement around the still figure of Venus. In the stupendous group of the Graces (plate 66), we see something else happen: the line vibrates subtly and continuously in a kind of full choral effect of undulations. The movement seems to become perpetual, increasing by the whirling of veils around the bodies as they now adhere, now float apart to reveal the shapes of the nudes beneath them (plate 67). Thus the musical line continues from one candid image to the other. The melody reaches a crescendo in the upward entwining of the fingers, and then subsides as the tension derived from Pollaiuolo relaxes in the figure of Mercury, who gazes toward the sky.

The music of this painting is inherent in its composition. Here, the line, not the play of enclosed volumes in perspective, articulates the structure. The picture is not taken in by the eye, it is read, or better sung, by following the line as it unfolds from right to left. Unity is created by the succession of images in time, just as in poetry and music. And an essential element, moreover, of this musical rendition of pictorial idioms is the perfect synthesis of line and volume. Botticelli's line is never purely arabesque; it does not deny the form. Rather, it resolves the movement of the volumes decoratively. Thus the image is fixed at the ideal point in time when the action passes over to imagery, and thus is born the timeless action of a Botticelli painting. Reality is transformed into image, history into myth. Classic reminiscence, which recent criticism tends to deny, perhaps out of fear of reducing the artist's originality, is perfectly relevant to this mythic conception of reality. Venus stands as isolated as an ancient statue, and her pose recalls a Greek Aphrodite, even if modified (as Gombrich says) by a gesture typical of a Virgin Annunciate. But here again this typological detail reflects the union of matter and spirit, of the senses and morality, which is the basis of the allegory. The perfect rhythm of the Graces echoes the marble sculpture Piccolomini placed in the Library of the Duomo in Siena. The distant sound of ancient modes can be heard around the new work, enriching it.

The tragic events of April 1478, gave Botticelli the opportunity of painting the conspirators who had been hanged beside the Palazzo Vecchio. He must have looked for suggestions in the frescoes by Andrea del Castagno on the tower of the Palazzo Podestà. Castagno's impact on Botticelli, and a sign of the artist's capacity to absorb new impressions, can be seen in the *St Augustine* in the Church of Ognissanti (plate 78). The heroic power—derived from Castagno—of that architectonic massing of plastic planes is realized by the incisive and tense outlines. The line suspends and holds immobile the mass which would tend to turn with the turn of the volumes and the opposite movement of the arms. The space itself, rendered in unusually sharp perspective for Botticelli, is firmly limited by the wall of the cell and springs toward the foreground with an intensity measured by the plasticity of the objects. The mass of the figure is blocked and restrained; the suffering humanity of the image becomes timeless, held fast to the thin line which divides the individual from the universal idea of the thoughtful hero. This sense of religious heroism is repeated in the splendid *St Thomas Aquinas* in Zurich (plate 82) and in the very strong *San Martino Annunciation* (plate 80), which Botticelli painted in the spring of 1481.

Botticelli must have been at the height of his fame, because that same summer Pope Sixtus IV called him to Rome, along with a few other Florentine and Umbrian artists, to decorate his Chapel in the Vatican. The task was extremely complicated. Botticelli had to paint a series of parallel episodes that would symbolize more than narrate the ideological unity between the Old and New Testaments. Botticelli certainly was not inexperienced in allegorical representation, and, as the *Primavera* proves, his imagination was impelled by the problems inherent in it. The spiritual meaning of the

27

figures he was to paint increased the detachment he felt was necessary between the image and a realistic rendering. But here the problem was aggravated by the fact that profound stories had to be told in monumental terms, set in naturalistic surroundings, because the viewers would not be the *élite* of Florentine humanists, but scores of pilgrims. Thus in the *Temptation of Christ* (plates 92–99), his efforts to harmonize the large, naturalistic space with the horizontal development of the figures along the picture plane, are clear. The figures assume a natural fullness which makes the linear rhythm less evident. On the other hand the rhythm is too disorganized and too frequently interrupted by unjustified pauses to be unified stylistically. There are none the less a number of striking portraits (plates 96–99) and splendid details, like the woman carrying firewood (plate 95), which are touched by the same musical grace that characterizes the *Primavera*. Or there is the group of figures behind the priest (plate 94) where the rhythm of the line is restrictive and almost strained, but eases in the subtler features of the boy with the curly hair. In the *Punishment of Korah* (plates 100–105), the scenographic buildings in the background, against a landscape as airy as any by Perugino, do not blend well with the grouping of the figures. They too seem to be implicated in the mere gestures of drama, and do not succeed, therefore, in becoming the ideal images so central to Botticelli's vision. The saving merit, again, is the vigorous portraiture (plates 103–105) or the charming ships moored to the fantastic docks, against a sea shot through with strange reflections (plate 101).

The fresco, *Scenes from the Life of Moses*, is exceptional, however, in that the compositional unity is achieved by enclosing the diagonal movement of the landscape in the angular and juxtaposed development of the figures, where tension is finally spent in the rustic daughters of Jethro (plate 88) in the center of the picture. The dramatic content here loses all naturalistic weight by moving along with a linear rhythm which joins figures and landscape in its lively course. Time, in fact, and not space, is Botticelli's muse. His imagination functions best whenever he can release the image from the corporality of space and allow it free play along the ideal or musical lines of time.

While in Rome, according to the sources, Botticelli also painted the *Adoration of the Magi*, which has been identified as the work now in Washington (plates 108–111). The interrupted and angular linear rhythm corresponds, although in a simpler structure, to the rhythm in the *Moses*. There is expressive immediacy in its painful anxiety.

Botticelli's stay in Rome was brief. His presence in Florence is documented in the summer of 1482. He committed himself to some work in the Palazzo Vecchio, but he never carried it out. About this time he was probably commissioned by Lorenzo the Magnificent to do some paintings for Villa Spadaletto near Volterra. But even if we no longer have the works in the Palazzo Vecchio or in the Villa Spadaletto, we can see that Botticelli's stay in Rome had its effect from the frescoes in the Villa Tornabuoni (plates 116–124) and particularly from the *Pallas and the Centaur* (plates 113–115). There is probably no other work by Botticelli in which the agreement between the unfolding of the line and the rounding of the volumes is so complete, nor can we see elsewhere such personal and even intense absorption in the ancient world. The Centaur's head (plate 114), for instance, imitates a Roman sarcophagus, and the figure of Athena has the proportions and stance of a Graeco-Roman statue against a background of ordered and solid architecture of distinctly Roman character.

But more relevant is the classical quality of the entire composition.

The fact that the line defines the turning volumes rather freely indicates that the artist found here an unusual point of balance between the natural concreteness of the figure and the ideal of the image, just as the landscape repeats the linear musicality by the way the space is carefully delineated by the rocks and the rectangle of the field, by the winding of the river and the bend of the hills against the clear marine horizon. So precise is the relationship between the form and the allegorical content of the painting that we can readily understand why recent scholarship interprets it as the reconciliation between reason and instinct, the twin components of man's soul.

With this great work, which stands as the most humanistic of Botticelli's *œuvre*, we consider it opportune to close this first chapter of his life as man and as artist. We do so just when new anxieties, and new causes intervene to upset that great balance and to evoke from his imagination other less foreseeable and more moving masterpieces.

BIOGRAPHICAL NOTES

1445. Born in Florence, the son of Mariano di Vanni Filipepi, a tanner, who lived in the Santa Maria Novella quarter (at least in 1457). This birthdate is derived from a fiscal document dated March 1, 1447 (Mesnil), in which Sandro is said to be two years old, and confirmed by another declaration, dated February 28, 1458, in which Sandro is indicated as being thirteen. Before Horne discovered this last document, Botticelli's birthdate was given as 1447, on the basis of a declaration to the Registry in 1480 (published by Gaye), in which his age is stated as thirty-three. Obviously we should put greater store on the older documents.

1458. In the declaration to the Registry, the old Filipepi states: "My son Sandro is thirteen years old, is reading, and is unhealthy . . .", implying that he is at school. In place of the Italian *legere* (reading), some scholars read *legare* (to set jewels), especially Mesnil, and claim that the boy was working as an apprentice to a goldsmith. But in that case, his father would have said "he is at the goldsmith's," or at least would have written the verb with an *h* as *leghare*. Thus the boy was still studying at thirteen, an unusual education for the times. The same document informs us that among the numerous members of the family, the most wealthy is the eldest brother, John, "a pawn-broker," nicknamed Botticello, or "Little Cask." The fact that the name passed to Sandro must mean, as Horne has correctly pointed out that his brother, more than his father, was responsible for raising the boy.

1465–67. Vasari's report that Botticelli was a student of Fra Filippo Lippi, and the existence of a series of panels painted by Botticelli, which copy Lippi's *Madonna and Child with St John the Baptist* (plates 1, 125, 126), and datable around 1465 or shortly after, lead us to suppose that Botticelli was an apprentice in Lippi's workshop during this time; that is, until Lippi moved to Spoleto.

1467–68 *ca*. We can ausume that Botticelli went to Verrocchio's workshop after Lippi's departure from Florence.

1470. Botticelli has his own workshop, according to the memoirs of Benedetto Dei, which Horne read.

1470, AUGUST 18. Finishes the *Fortitude* (see comment on plate 20) for the tribunal of the Arte della Mercanzia.

1472. Botticelli's name appears in the *Red Book* of the Company of St Luke, charged with various contributions.

1472. From the same *Red Book* we learn that Filippino Lippi is an apprentice in Botticelli's workshop.

1473. Other contributions to the Company of St Luke.

1474, JANUARY. January 1473 (Florentine style; therefore 1474) could be clearly read on the now lost frame for the *St Sebastian* of Santa Maria Maggiore. It should be considered as being painted between the end of 1473 and the beginning of the next year, since the *Anonimo Gaddiano* cites the work, adding that "he did it in January 1473." This certainly must be the *St Sebastian* in Berlin (see comment on plate 45).

1474. We read in the documents published by Tanfani Centofanti, by Supino and by Horne that Botticelli went to Pisa toward the end of January to look into the frescoes he was to execute for the cemetery alongside the first eight Benozzo had already finished. Botticelli had to prove his capabilities by painting an *Assumption* in the Chapel of the Incoronata in the Duomo in Pisa. He worked on this fresco from July to September 20, 1474. Vasari remembers that the fresco was incomplete. Evidently the Pisans did not appreciate Botticelli as much as they did Benozzo, and so he was not allowed to paint the frescoes for the cemetery. The fresco in the Duomo was destroyed in 1583.

1475, JANUARY 28. Botticelli finishes a standard with the figure of Pallas Athena for Giuliano de' Medici to carry into the tourney on this date, according to Poggi's unquestionable thesis (1902). The standard is listed with Botticelli's name in the inventory taken at Lorenzo the Magnificent's death.

1478. He paints a fresco over the door of the Dogana in the Bargello of the conspirator hanged in the Pazzi conspiracy. This was executed between April 26 (the day of the conspiracy) and July 21 (the day he was paid). The fresco was destroyed, along with Castagno's fresco of hanged traitors on the Palazzo Podestà (the Albizi conspiracy), on November 14, 1494, after Piero de' Medici fled Florence (Horne).

1480. In competition with Ghirlandaio, he paints the fresco of *St Augustine* in the Church of Ognissanti (see comment on plate 78).

1481, APRIL–MARCH. Frescoes the *Annunciation* (now detached) in the vestibule of San Martino delle Scala (see comment on plate 80).
   In his statement to the Registry, Botticelli's father declared: "Sandro, son of Mariano, aged thirty-three is a painter and works at home when he wants to."

1481-82. From the summer of 1481 until spring 1482 (or August at the latest), he is in Rome where he is working on the Sistine Chapel frescoes (see comment on plates 87, 92, 100).

1482. His father dies and is buried in the Church of Ognissanti.
   On October 5, the men in charge of the Signoria, referring to a decision made the preceding August, make an agreement with Ghirlandaio, Botticelli, Perugino, Piero del Pollaiuolo and Biagio

d'Antonio Tucci to decorate the Hall of the Lilies (or Priors) with frescoes. Botticelli was to paint, along with Ghirlandaio, the wall toward the audience room of the Priors. The frescoes were never done; Ghirlandaio only painted a *St Zenobius*, which still exists.

On November 25, Botticelli pays a fee of ten *soldi* to the Company of St Luke.

1483. He prepares the drawings and supervises his students while they paint the four panels for *cassoni*, for the second marriage of Giannozzo Pucci, this time with Lucrezia Bini.

1483? He paints frescoes in the Villa Spadaletto near Volterra, which belongs to Lorenzo the Magnificent. Filippino Lippi, Perugino and Ghirlandaio are working on the same project. A letter datable a little after 1485 from an anonymous agent of Ludovico il Moro (published by Müller-Walde) confirms this: "All these above-mentioned masters have proved themselves in Pope Sixtus's Chapel, except Filippino. But everyone then at Messer Lorenzo's Spadaletto, and the palm is ambiguous" (meaning that they were all worthy of commendation).

BOTTICELLI'S PAINTINGS

Color Plate I

DISCOVERY OF THE MURDER OF HOLOFERNES. Detail of plate 43.

Plate 1

MADONNA AND CHILD. *Panel, 87 × 60.* Florence, Museo dell'Ospedale degli Innocenti.* Traditionally attributed to Filippo Lippi (and included in Cavalcaselle's catalog of Lippi's works), the painting was reassigned to Botticelli by Ulmann (1893), followed by Bode (1921 and 1926), by Gamba (1932) and Berenson (1932). Van Marle (1931) and Bettini (1942), have doubts, but Horne rejects the possibility outright along with A. Venturi, who assigns it to Filippo Lippi's school, and, less emphatically, Mesnil (1938). Other scholars (Yashiro, etc.) are silent on the matter, omitting the panel from their catalogs. Here, as in the works given in plates 125–126, we have a rather academic variation of Filippo Lippi's *Madonna and Angels* in the Uffizi (1465); the minor quality of the work would ordinarily discourage attributing it to Botticelli, if it were not for the unmistakable, even if germinal, signs in the illustration and in the stylistic quirks of his more mature works. It is reasonable to suppose this was an exercise he did in Lippi's workshop as a young apprentice. Otherwise we would have to imagine an anonymous follower of Lippi, whose other works have been lost and who was influenced in turn by the young Botticelli (no document hints at the possibility). Where we might consider the work immature for a talented painter in his twenties, we should recall that Botticelli began to paint relatively late—he was still studying at thirteen. The works attributable to him before the documented *Fortitude* (1470) reveal a slow and laborious development.

This painting, if not all three *Madonnas*, might be considered a first attempt, datable around 1465. The painting was restored in about 1890, but is quite faded because of earlier efforts at cleaning it. Although Gamba finds Pollaiuolo's influence in the colors, we can only detect Lippi's influence.

Plate 2

MADONNA AND CHILD WITH ANGEL. *Panel, 110 × 70. Ajaccio, Musée Fesch.* Formerly in the collection of Cardinal Fesch (1839). Published for the first time by L. Vertova (1948) after Berenson had spoken of it as one of Botticelli's first works. Longhi confirmed the attribution orally, and so did Laclotte (1956). The attempt to recreate a new rhythm for Lippi's composition succeeds here for the first time, despite some uncertainties, especially in the lower part of the figure. Datable therefore somewhat later than 1465.

Plate 3

MADONNA OF THE LOGGIA. *Panel, 72 × 50. Florence, Uffizi Gallery.*

* All dimensions are given in centimeters.

Originally anonymous, it came from the Chamber of Commerce in 1784, and was later assigned as a Botticelli in the inventories. The attribution was denied by Morelli (1890), followed by other scholars. A. Venturi was uncertain, since at first he accepted it among Botticelli's youthful works (1911), but then omitted it from the catalog (1925). In any case, while Van Marle attributed it to "Sandro's friend," (1931), Gamba (1932 and 1936) and Berenson reclaimed it for the young artist.

Bettini accepted the attribution to Botticelli, dating it to 1467–70, but Mesnil rejected it, claiming it was the work of an eclectic follower of Lippi, Verrocchio and Botticelli himself. Although the painting has some aspects that are slightly different from the artist's usual work, which Berenson explained as someone else's help in finishing it, I do not think we can reject the painting during this period of tentative judgments and further research into the young artist's achievements. The painting is fundamentally in Lippi's style, but the Child's body reveals an effort to lyricize Lippi's forms. Probably painted around 1467.

Plate 4

GUIDI MADONNA. *Panel, 73 × 40. Paris, Louvre.* Formerly in the Guidi Collection in Faenza, it was sold in Rome at Sangiorgi's in 1902 and taken to the Louvre by Schlichting. It was published as a youthful work derived from Fra Filippo's *Madonna* in Munich by A. Venturi (1902 and 1907), but later the critic changed his mind and attributed it to the artist's school (1925). It was accepted as an autograph painting by Gebhardt (1908), by Yashiro (1929), who had first doubted it, and by Van

Marle (1931). P. Jamot said it was a school product (1920), while L. Venturi claimed Fra Filippo painted it when he was in Prato. Everyone dates it before 1470. The painter probably had Lippi's *Madonna* in mind, as well as Verrocchio's *Madonna* in Berlin (No. 104A), which in turn, according to Pudelko (1936), is derived from Fra Filippo's *Madonna* in Munich. We think it is by the young Botticelli, who was imitating Verrocchio. A probable date of around 1467–68.

Plate 5

MADONNA AND CHILD. *Panel, 72 × 52. Paris, Louvre.* In 1865 this was in the Campana Collection in the Louvre, then stored in Périgueux, and is now back in the Louvre. Traditionally attributed to Filippo Lippi, it is considered a product of the young Botticelli's school by Berenson (1932) and Pittaluga (1949). Laclotte assigns it to the artist himself around 1470. Unquestionably by Botticelli, it should be dated a year earlier, around 1468, because it is inspired by a Verrocchio influenced by Lippi, and is still far from the Verrocchio influenced by Pollaiuolo that we see in the *Fortitude*.

Plate 6

MADONNA AND CHILD WITH ST JOHN THE BAPTIST. *Panel, 85 × 62. Florence, Accademia.* From the Church of Santa Maria Nuova, where it was labeled as a Lippi, it was taken to the Uffizi in 1900, and in 1919, to the Accademia. Ulmann thought (1893) that the *Anonimo Gaddiano* referred to this panel ("a small panel in Santa Maria Nuova next to the central door . . ."), but this cannot be true since the passage is interpolated from the Petrei Codex (*Libro di Antonio Billi*) which clearly reads

"S. Maria *Novella*." The reference is obviously to the *Adoration of the Magi* (plate 52). Procacci attributes it to Botticelli (1951). Horne and A. Venturi think it is a school product, and other scholars are silent. The panel is not damaged by the extensive retouching, and from its reminiscences of Lippi and Verrocchio, we can date it about 1468.

Plate 7

MADONNA AND CHILD WITH ST JOHN THE BAPTIST. Detail: the Virgin's head.

Plate 8

MADONNA AND CHILD WITH ST JOHN. *Panel, 93 × 69. Paris, Louvre.* Cavalcaselle noted an affinity with Botticelli's coloring, even though he included this painting in Fra Filippo's school. Shortly after this, the Louvre called it a Botticelli in its catalog. Ulmann argued critically for the attribution (1893), and everyone agreed except A. Venturi (1925) and Berenson (1932), who both assign it to the workshop, and Yashiro (1925), who limits the attribution by saying it was finished in the workshop. Most of the scholars date it before 1470, but several date it afterwards. I think it was painted after 1470 because of its high quality. The painting has been retouched, but it is probably by Botticelli.

A study for the Angel in one of the *Madonnas* may be the *Head of a Youth* (circular drawing, diameter 7.5; London, British Museum) in ink and white lead on a deep rose background. Berenson first attributed it to "Sandro's friend," then to the young (but not too young) Botticelli. Popham and Pouncey accept the opinion. Given the distinct Lippi

touch in the drawing and type, the work should be dated before 1470.

Plate 9

MADONNA AND CHILD WITH ST JOHN. Detail of the Virgin and Child.

Plate 10

MADONNA AND CHILD WITH YOUTH. *Panel, 85 × 66. New York, Duveen Collection.* It was originally in the Austen Collection (Uorsmonden, Kentucky) and labeled a Botticelli. L. Venturi (1933), Gamba (1936) and Mesnil (1938) support the attribution. Yashiro, on the other hand, considers it a copy of the workshop *Madonna* in the Féral-Epstein Collection, Chicago (see Attributed Paintings, plate 128), but Van Marle assigns it to "Sandro's friend." Quite close to the *Madonna of the Rose Arbor*, and therefore datable around 1467–68.

Plate 11

MADONNA AND CHILD. *Panel, 74 × 56. Washington, National Gallery, Mellon Collection.* Formerly in the Corsini Gallery in Florence, it went to the Duveen Brothers in New York, and then to Washington. It was considered a Filippino Lippi, but Bode (1893) assigned it to Botticelli. Other critics immediately seconded the attribution. The catalog *Duveen Pictures in Public Collections in America*, 1941, carried it as a Botticelli. Berenson, and then Van Marle, assigned it to "Sandro's friend," and A. Venturi to Botticelli's school. When the painting went to the Mellon Collection, it was cleaned, revealing clearly that it is by Botticelli, no matter how many critics fail to mention it. As Bode observed, Lippi's influences blend with Verrocchio's. Painted around 1468.

Plate 12a

MADONNA AND CHILD. *Panel, 70 × 48. London, National Gallery.* Originally from the Zambrini Collection in Imola and considered a Fra Filippo. A controversial work; critics have identified it as by someone intermediate between Botticelli and Filippino, or by an anonymous follower of Verrocchio or by a Florentine under Fra Filippo's influence. Berenson (1932) considered it as a product of the young Botticelli's school, while Davies thinks it is an imitation done outside the school. Only Van Marle (with some doubts) and Mesnil (positively) think it is Botticelli's, but many scholars are silent on the matter. This painting tends toward Lippi, while the *Madonna* in Naples, of which Yashiro considers it a copy, is heavily Verrocchian. Probably painted shortly before the Naples *Madonna*.

Plate 12b

MADONNA AND CHILD WITH ANGELS. *Panel, 100 × 71. Naples, National Galleries of Capodimonte.*

It was in the Farnese Palace in Rome, and carried in the inventory of 1697 as a "Fra Filippino [*sic*]." Cavalcaselle judged it to be by an imitator of Fra Filippo and of Botticelli, but Bode assigned it to Botticelli, followed by Ulmann. Berenson thought it by "Sandro's friend" in 1899. Recently, Davies seems inclined to accept it as autograph. Most of the critics date the painting before 1470, but L. Venturi puts it about 1470, while Bettini about 1472 and Yashiro, 1474. Again judging from the Lippi and Verrocchio elements, I would date it around 1468–69.

Plate 13a

MADONNA AND CHILD WITH ANGELS. *Panel, 107 × 75. Strasbourg, Musée des Beaux-Arts.* Bode was the first to attribute it to Botticelli and a number of critics agree. But Berenson rejects it, terming it a workshop painting, and so does Mesnil who finds in it a mixture of Verrocchian and Botticellian elements. Many critics ignore it. Although retouched and weakened, the painting is probably Botticelli's, done just when Verrocchio's influence was beginning to dominate.

Plate 13b

MADONNA AND CHILD WITH ANGELS. *Panel, 69.5 × 50. London, National Gallery.* In the middle of the nineteenth century it was in the Callcott Collection, and after passing through several English collections, it went to the National Gallery as part of the Salting Bequest. Ulmann, on Bode's suggestion, attributed it to Botticelli (revised edition, 1961) ascribes it to the "Florentine School" and Van Marle ascribes it to Verrocchio's school. Gamba, Bettini and I have all accepted it as autograph, while Mesnil, Davies and Water-house disagree. The general dis-agreement is due to the high proportion of Verrocchian elements in this painting, although the theme is analogous to the Strasbourg *Madonna* (see comment on plate 13a). In fact, it would almost seem that Verrocchio or one of his assistants painted the metallic and precious polish of the Angel's garments, the uprightness of the trees and the aureole which repeats the line of the neck. We have to consider that Botticelli may have worked with Verrocchio around 1469, and that this painting could have been done in Verrocchio's workshop with some help from Verrocchio.

Plate 14

MADONNA AND CHILD WITH ANGELS. *Panel, 62 × 42. Paris, Louvre.* Once attributed to Filippo Lippi's school, the painting was first assigned to Botticelli by Bode in 1887, followed by Ulmann (1893), who pairs it with the painting in plate 15. Sirén, however, ascribed it to an anonymous painter he calls "The Master of the Oriental Scarf." Both Venturi and Berenson consider it a school product. Several critics insist it is an autograph Botticelli. Commentary on this painting has always brought out its Verrocchio-like elements, but certainly the sharper inflexions of line already tend toward Pollaiuolo. Stylistically, it begins to approach the *Fortitude* (see plate 20), and so we date it around 1469–70.

Plate 15

MADONNA IN GLORY WITH SERA-PHIM. *Panel, 120 × 65. Florence, Uffizi Gallery.* In the inventory of 1784, it was carried as an anonymous painting. Bode ascribed it to the young Botticelli, and several critics agree: Ulmann, Schmarsow, Ya-shiro, Van Marle, Gamba, Berenson, L. Venturi, Mesnil and Bettini. A. Venturi ascribes it to Lippi's school. Other critics are silent. Here again the Verrocchian influence has been absorbed more thoroughly, and the dating should be about 1469–70.

Plate 16

MADONNA OF THE ROSE ARBOR. *Panel, 124 × 64. Florence, Uffizi Gallery.* The panel comes from the Chamber of Commerce (eighteenth century), and was later identified as a Botticelli. Morelli judged it a "bastard workshop piece." Ulmann, however, claimed it for the young Botticelli, and Bode agreed (1893), adding later that it was probably painted around 1469–70. Most critics agree, except Horne and A. Venturi, who both fail to record it. A notable work, quite close to the *Fortitude* and datable around 1469–70.

Color Plate II

JUDITH WITH THE HEAD OF HOLOFERNES.

Plate 17

MADONNA OF THE ROSE ARBOR. Detail: the Virgin's head.

Plate 18

PORTRAIT OF A YOUNG MAN. *Panel, 53.3 × 36.2. Santa Monica, California, Barbara Hutton Collection.* Appearing for the first time in a show of early works at the Royal Academy in London in 1886, it was ascribed to Fiorenzo di Lorenzo (in the *Bulletin of the Metropolitan Museum of Art*, 1917; Sirén and Brockwell, *Catalogue of a Loan Exhibition of Italian Primitives. Klein-berger Galleries,* New York, 1917;

Belvedere, 1922; etc.). Berenson attributed it to Botticelli in 1932, followed by Gamba, while more recent criticism has been non-committal. Although retouched to a degree, the portrait seems clearly a Botticelli of this period. The sky and landscape (with small figures of peasants at work) are of the type made popular by Baldovinetti and quickly taken up by Pollaiuolo. The elements appear a few years later, with a more distinct Pollaiuolo accent, in the *Portrait of a Man with a Medal* in the Uffizi (plate 47).

Plate 19

PORTRAIT OF A YOUTH. *Panel, 51 × 33.7. Florence, Pitti Palace.* The old inventories carried this portrait as by Andrea del Castagno, and Burckhardt (1855), Cavalcaselle, and Morelli accepted the attribution. A. Venturi at first (1891) ascribed it to Botticelli, but later to Filippo Lippi's school (1925). A number of critics, including Berenson (with reservations), Rusconi, Bettini, Collobi Ragghianti and C. Francini, agree on Botticelli. Despite the silence of the other critics, this portrait is unquestionably the master's, as the cleaning in 1935 reconfirmed. Lippi's forms here have gained in monumentality and vigor as Verrocchio's influence is felt, with perhaps some influence of Pollaiuolo visible. We would not say with Kroeber that there are signs of some contact with Memling. Datable probably around 1469–70.

Plate 20

FORTITUDE. *Panel, 167 × 87. Florence, Uffizi Gallery.* This is the first cited and documented work, and therefore the pivot for reconstructing the activities of the young Botticelli. Albertini (1510), the Petrei Codex, the *Anonimo Gaddiano* and Vasari (1550 and 1568) agree that Botticelli painted the *Fortitude* along with the six other *Virtues* for the tribunal in the Mercanzia, the work by Piero del Pollaiuolo. Horne found that the building housing the Arte della Mercanzia was in the Piazza della Signoria, at the corner of Via de' Gondi. The *Virtues* were painted on the backs of the single seats along the tribunal, or more probably, on the wooden border around the room. From there, they were transferred to the Uffizi, where they were recorded by Cinelli in 1677. In 1777, when the Arte della Mercanzia was suppressed, the panels were put in storage and not exhibited again until 1861. Mesnil discovered some documents in 1903 which confirmed the other sources and gave a precise date: August 18, 1469, when the Arte della Mercanzia commissioned Piero del Pollaiuolo to do a *Charity*. Verrocchio was probably competing, and we have his drawing for a *Faith* (Gabinetto degli Uffizi, No. 208E). On December 18, all the *Virtues* were entrusted to Piero, either because his drawings pleased the authorities more than Verrocchio's, or because Verrocchio failed to submit his in time. In August 1470, Pollaiuolo finished two of the *Virtues*. In May 1470, Tommaso Soderini, the new head of the Arte, and influential because of his friendship with Lorenzo de' Medici, succeeded in having two of the *Virtues* assigned to Botticelli. On August 18, Sandro was paid for his panel *Fortitude*. But the other *Virtue* was given back to Pollaiuolo to do, probably because he protested. This incident probably figures in the protest that representatives of the artists made in 1471 to the Arte dei Medici e Speziali, in which they ask that a work already assigned to an artist should not be reassigned to another.

We agree with Yashiro, Bettini and Argan that the painting is marked by a balance between Verrocchio's and Pollaiuolo's influence. It is questionable still whether the young Botticelli, after his initial experience with Lippi, turned toward Pollaiuolo first, and then to Verrocchio, or the reverse. The chronology we are developing here supports the second possibility.

Plate 21

FORTITUDE. Detail: the bust.

Plate 22

ALTARPIECE OF THE CONVERTITE (?). *Panel, 170 × 194. Florence, Uffizi Gallery.* Sixteenth-century sources, the *Libro di Antonio Billi* (Petrei Codex), the *Anonimo Gaddiano,* Vasari and Borghini (1584), mention among Botticelli's works a panel in the Church of the Augustinian Nuns of St Elizabeth of the Converted, a convent founded in the fourteenth century for penitent prostitutes. The painting was recorded in the church or the convent until 1802, but none of the writers who mention it describes its theme. So it is a pure hypothesis to identify the *Altarpiece* with this panel, which includes the Madonna and Child enthroned among SS John the Baptist, Francis, Mary Magdalen, Catherine of Alexandria, Cosmas and Damian and which came from the Church of Sant'-Ambrogio all'Accademia, and went from there, in 1946, to its present location. Gamba suggested it is the *Altarpiece of the Convertite* in 1930–36, and though frequently accepted, his judgment has been questioned (Mesnil). A favorable indication is the presence of Mary Magdalen, the patron of repentant prostitutes; unfavorable is the absence of either St Elizabeth, the titular of the convent, or St Augustine, patron of the Order. The faces of Cosmas and Damian resemble Lorenzo and Giuliano de' Medici, but this might indicate an homage to the city rulers, or a token of their having commissioned the panel or both. Yashiro's proposal is even more doubtful; that is, to identify the Fareham *Trinity* as the *Altarpiece.* If this panel is the *Altarpiece,* we still have the problem of dating it. Horne's suggestion that it is related to the building of a new Chapel in St Elizabeth's around 1491 is not at all necessary. An analysis of the style has produced different opinions, mainly because, until a few years ago, repainting (which was probably done in the sixteenth century) had considerably altered its appearance. Critics have dated it, for the most part, after 1470, but Yashiro put it near the *Fortitude,* around 1470. As in the *Fortitude,* the Verrocchio-like impression is given energy by the twisting of the two doctors and the unrest of St Catherine, which derive from Pollaiuolo.

Plate 23

ALTARPIECE OF THE CONVERTITE. Detail: the Child and St Damian.

Plate 24

ALTARPIECE OF THE CONVERTITE. Detail: Mary Magdalen.

Plate 25

ALTARPIECE OF THE CONVERTITE. Detail: St Catherine of Alexandria.

Plate 26

CHRIST TEACHING. *Panel, 18 × 42. Philadelphia, Johnson Collection.*

This and the three panels reproduced in plates 27–29 were put on sale in the antique market in Florence in 1910. After they were acquired for the Johnson Collection, Berenson and Horne identified them as Botticelli's works, dating them a little later than 1470, and going so far as to identify them as parts of the lost *Altarpiece of the Convertite*. Bode, however, noted the late style of the panels, the vibrant, intense period about the time of Savonarola, and dated them about 1490. Yashiro claimed the panels formed the predella of the Fareham *Trinity* (see Attributed Paintings), which he had identified as the *Altarpiece of the Convertite*. Bode and A. Venturi accepted Yashiro's claim, but dated the works much later, in the 80s and 90s. I incline to associate the panels with the *Altarpiece of the Convertite* (see comment on plate 22), whether it is or is not the real altarpiece, and date them around 1470. The very perceptible vibration of the line, which has led many critics to date the work late, is related, on the other hand, to the monumental quality of the Lippi-Verrocchio tradition, and is a sign of youthful hesitation in the composition. The vibration should be interpreted as a timid approach to Pollaiuolo, and is matched not only in the two *Adoration of the Magi* in London (plates 32 and 38), but also in the miniature figures we find in the panels painted during this period; for instance, the one in the Hutton Collection (plate 18).

Plate 27

FEAST IN THE HOUSE OF SIMON. *Panel, 18 × 42. Philadelphia, Johnson Collection.* See comment on plate 26.

Plate 28

"NOLI ME TANGERE." *Panel, 18 ×* *42. Philadelphia, Johnson Collection.* See comment on plate 26.

Plate 29

LAST MOMENTS OF MARY MAGDALEN. *Panel, 18 × 42. Philadelphia, Johnson Collection.* The events in the panel are actually part of the legend of St Mary of Egypt, but were frequently attributed to Mary Magdalen at that time. See comment on plate 26.

Plate 30

MADONNA AND CHILD. *Fresco, about 70 × 250. Florence, Church of the Annunziata, Sacristy of the Virgin.* Part of a much larger fresco which decorated the Chapel of the Virgin of the Angels, which used to adjoin the Church of the Annunziata, but was later transformed into a sacristy. Originally located much lower, where the main door is now. The draperies and the figure of the Virgin are original, except for some retouching. The Child was totally repainted. Gamba discovered the fresco as a Botticelli in 1934, and he dates it convincingly in the artist's Verrocchio period, around 1470–71.

Plate 31

ANNUNCIATION. *Panel, 8.2 × 12.6. Glens Falls, New York, Hyde Collection.* L. Venturi noted this as a youthful work in 1933. Most critics date it around 1471, bringing it close to the supposed *Altarpiece of the Convertite*. Yashiro dates it later (1474) and so, apparently, does Berenson, who did not put the usual sign after this painting in the index, indicating a youthful work. Undoubtedly the correct date is the earliest, because of its relation with the predella in Philadelphia and its own strong Verrocchio quality. The vision here is original, so much so that certain aspects (i.e. the Angel) resemble the typical forms of a Lorenzo di Credi.

Plates 32–33

ADORATION OF THE MAGI. *Panel, 50 × 139. London, National Gallery.* From the Orlandini Collection in Florence, it went to the Lombardi-Baldi Collection in 1845, where it was attributed to Filippino, and finally to London in 1875. Although Cavalcaselle continued to consider the panel a Filippino (1864), Morelli reascribed it to Botticelli in 1873, and later criticism has agreed with this. Some scholars consider it Sandro's first or at least very early work, including Horne, Yashiro, A. Venturi, Gamba, and Bettini. Others think it was probably painted a year or two later. Judgment is difficult, not only because the cleaning in 1940 revealed that the painting is considerably damaged from past cleanings, but also because of contrasting stylistic features. On the one hand, the uncertainty of a rather Lippi-influenced design would place the work among Botticelli's earliest. But many figures, especially on the right and left sides, are related to the more vigorous, later Pollaiuolo period, after the *Fortitude*. On the left and in the center, however, the heads and the excessive drapery are weak. The incongruities may be explained by a collaboration between Botticelli and Filippino around 1472, when—according to our records—Filippino (who was thirteen at this time) was working in Sandro's *bottega*. The composition was probably projected by the precocious Filippino, and Botticelli intervened by painting a number of figures and repainting other parts (the cleaning revealed several *pentimenti*). The group on the left, with its vigorous figures of horses, and a little lower the three

heads which are comparable to the *Discovery of the Murder of Holofernes* (plate 43), and then the dwarf, all reveal Botticelli's touch at the time when he was imitating Pollaiuolo; that is, after 1470. A little higher in the confused composition of the same group, one can see a more detailed, subtle and vibrant rendering of the typical Botticelli figure—and here Filippino did the greater part. In the group to the right of the pillar, the heads with their careful, psychological representation are also Filippino's work, and so is the drapery, with the exception of the last figure on the right so typically Botticellian, an example of the distended and loose design that mark Filippino's early works. Botticelli did the kneeling King, the figure looking at the star and his genuflecting companion. The dominant artist on the left side was Botticelli; indeed the shepherds already show the strong Pollaiuolo character of Botticelli's next period.

Plate 34

ADORATION OF THE MAGI. Detail: the kneeling King and the Virgin and Child.

Plate 35

MADONNA OF THE EUCHARIST. *Panel, 84 × 65. Boston, Isabella Gardner Museum.* The title derives from the wheat and the grapes (bread and wine, the symbols of the Sacrament) which the Angel presents to the Virgin. In 1908, it went from the Chigi Palace in Rome to the Gardner Collection. After Morelli (1891), Ulmann and A. Venturi (1896) confirmed the attribution to Botticelli, the rest of the critics agreed. Everyone except Schmarsow places it among the artist's youthful works, most probably around 1472. The accents here are dominantly Pollaiu-oloesque, and so I think the painting should be separated by a year or two from the far less mature series of Verrocchio-like *Madonnas* (plates 12b, 13b, etc.), to which this *Madonna* has frequently been compared. There is a copy in the Musée Condé in Chantilly, which Waagen (*Suppl.*, I) and Rio (*Art Chrétien*, II) consider autograph, but Ulmann and subsequent criticism reject the possibility. Post's interpretation of the allegory as Neoplatonic is probably correct: the ethereal, transfigured beauty of the image corresponds to Ficino's doctrines which Girolamo Benivieni wrote of in his poetry. Man reaches the adoration of beauty by stages: from the physical love of a woman, to spiritual love of her and thus to heavenly beauty which she reflects. Finally he achieves the ideal of perfect beauty, which is God.

Plate 36

PORTRAIT OF ESMERALDA BAN-DINELLI (?). *Panel, 65 × 41. London, Victoria and Albert Museum.* The panel was once part of the Pourtalès Collection, and then belonged to the poet-painter, Dante Gabriel Rossetti, who, it appears, retouched it. On the window-sill can be read "Smeralda of M. Bandinelli, the wife of Vi. Bandinelli," who would have been Esmeralda Donati, Viviano's wife (from documents dating from 1450 on), the mother of the goldsmith Michelangiolo Bandinelli, and grandmother of Baccio Bandinelli, the sculptor (born 1488). But since Bandinelli assumed this name in 1530, the inscription was considered apocryphal and historically worthless. Berenson considered the work as "Sandro's friend's," and both Yashiro and A. Venturi judged it a school product. A number of

other critics (Bettini is noncommittal) accept the painting as Botticelli's. There is some discussion of the probable date, ranging from 1470 to 1482. L. Venturi dates it around 1478, close to the *Primavera* and Mesnil considers it a youthful work. The Verrocchio-like aspects, although modified by the beginnings of Pollaiuolo's influence, and its affinity with the supposed *Altarpiece of the Convertite*, lead us to assume it was executed around 1471.

Plate 37

PORTRAIT OF A WOMAN AS ST CATHERINE. *Panel, 81 × 53. Altenburg, Lindenau Museum.* Once considered as a Ghirlandaio, it was classified by Cavalcaselle as a work influenced by Piero della Francesca, Andrea del Castagno and Pollaiuolo. Schmarsow (1897) ascribed it to Botticelli and described the woman as Caterina Sforza, the daughter of Galeazzo, who married Giovanni di Pierfrancesco de' Medici in 1497. The scholar referred to a medallion and a portrait in fresco in the Feo Chapel in San Biagio, Forlì. The attributes of St Catherine assumed by the sitter are either a tribute to the Saint or an indication that the sitter's discontent with her portrait caused the painter to change the picture to a sacred image. The painting was executed in Rome in 1481, when Caterina married her first husband Riario. Kroeber accepted this theory. The critics who accept it as Botticelli's work agree for the most part that it is a youthful effort because of the unquestionable Verrocchio and Pollaiuolo traits. Thus the identification as Caterina Sforza would be mistaken, since she was born in 1463, but Gamba's theory that the woman is a Sforza none the less is more probable; that is, the Duchess

Bona or some other member of the family. Gamba thinks the painting was done on the occasion of Galeazzo Sforza's visit to Lorenzo the Magnificent in March 1471.

Plate 38

TONDO: THE ADORATION OF THE MAGI. *Panel, diameter 131.5. London, National Gallery.* Milanesi thought this was the *tondo* of the *Epiphany* Vasari had mentioned as being in the Pucci family. Davies's research (1951) has confirmed the hypothesis. The painting, which went to the National Gallery in 1878 after belonging to several English collectors, was once in the Guicciardini Palace. The family probably came into possession of it in 1720, through a marriage with Luisa Ninfa de' Pucci, the niece of Cosimo (died 1707), who owned an *Epiphany*, three "arms" wide, according to a register of 1698. The Guicciardini inventory carried the painting as a Botticelli. Cavalcaselle ascribed the panel to Botticelli and subsequent criticism has been in full agreement. It is generally considered earlier than the more famous *Adoration* in the Uffizi, and opinion ranges from 1470 to 1476.

The young man in the foreground who turns to look at the viewer may be a self-portrait. The composition and most of the painting are Botticelli's, while some details may have been done by Filippino, especially the little heads in the background of the royal procession.

Plate 39

TONDO: THE ADORATION OF THE MAGI. Central detail: the Virgin and Child, and St Joseph.

Plate 40

TONDO: THE ADORATION OF

THE MAGI. Detail: peacock and landscape in upper right.

Color Plate III

PORTRAIT OF A MAN WITH A MEDAL.

Plate 41

TONDO: THE ADORATION OF THE MAGI. Detail: the procession of the Magi and landscape on the right.

Plate 42

TONDO: THE ADORATION OF THE MAGI. Detail: the procession of the Magi on the left.

Plate 43

DISCOVERY OF THE MURDER OF HOLOFERNES. *Panel, 31 × 25, Florence, Uffizi Gallery.* Borghini relates that this painting and *Judith with the Head of Holofernes* were given as gifts to Bianca Cappello, the bride of Francesco I, the Grand Duke of Tuscany, by Rodolfo Sirigatti. Antonio de' Medici, Bianca's son, inherited the paintings (cf. the inventory of the house on Via Larga, 1588: "a small picture, divided in half, making two smaller pictures . . ."), and after his death in 1632, the paintings went to their present location. Everyone agrees they are by Botticelli. Most of the critics think he painted them shortly after 1470, although others (Yashiro, Bettini) date them around 1467–68, or 1470 (Argan). Bettini explains such precocity by the presence of Mantegna in Tuscany in 1466–67 and his certain influence on the receptive Botticelli, especially with his own *Judith*, now lost, that was registered in the Medici inventory in 1492. This may be so, but all these considerations only serve to give us a limiting date. The definite point is the ~~decision~~ in favor of Pollaiuolo that the two paintings represent, and the foreshadowing, in the *Return of Judith,* of the musical linearity of the *Primavera.* The date of execution is certainly later than 1470, probably 1472.

Plate 44

JUDITH WITH THE HEAD OF HOLOFERNES. Detail: the landscape on the right.

Plate 45

ST SEBASTIAN. *Panel, 195 × 75. Berlin, Staaliche Museen.* Acquired with the Solly Collection in 1821, the panel was identified as by Antonio del Pollaiuolo until 1864, when Cavalcaselle ascribed it to Botticelli. Certainly identifiable with the painting mentioned in the *Anonimo Gaddiano:* ". . . in Santa Maria Maggiore there is a panel of San Bastiano by his hand, who is on a column, which he painted in January 1473." The anonymous author probably read the date on the now lost frame. We note that 1473 would be 1474 by our dating. Even Vasari recalls (1550) "a St Sebastian in Santa Maria Maggiore in Florence," painted by Botticelli. In the second edition of his *Lives,* he corrected the location by putting a period after the Saint's name. He goes on to cite a *Pietà* in Santa Maria Maggiore, and puts the *St Sebastian* in the Medici Palace along with a *Pallas.* Vasari probably took his information from the *Gaddiano* without verifying it, and later realized the report was not accurate. It is quite improbable that the panel was in the church in 1550 and then in the Medici Palace in 1568, when Vasari issued his second edition, because a reference to Lorenzo would be meaningless. There is no reason to doubt, in any case, the *Anonimo*

Gaddiano's attribution, which is now commonly accepted. Although critics have insisted on maintaining a relationship between Botticelli's *Sebastian* and the one by Pollaiuoli, now in London, Davies and Mesnil point out that the similarities are only generic. We have to acknowledge, however, that this panel marks a highpoint in Botticelli's use of the functional linearity which characterized Pollaiuolo's art. His use of Pollaiuolo's style, furthermore, is much more careful and more profound than his superficial borrowing from the sculptural plasticity of Verrocchio.

Plate 46

PORTRAIT OF A MEDICI. *Panel, 44 × 32. Formerly in Florence, Corsini Gallery.* The panel bore the name of Antonio del Pollaiuolo for a long time, until Morelli reascribed it to Botticelli in 1873. Critics have been in disagreement ever since. Berenson, A. Venturi and Ortolani think it is Botticelli's work. The painting seems quite altered under X-rays, but the best preserved parts —for instance, the hand, the ring and the sill with the flowers—have a vigor and transparency worthy of the master. The probable date is around 1474 (his Pollaiuolo period), or if we want to take account of the lessening of the linear tension, then 1475 would be more likely. Venturi claims that the diamond-pointed ring identifies the sitter as a member of the Medici family.

Plate 47

PORTRAIT OF A MAN WITH A MEDAL. *Panel, 57.5 × 44. Florence, Uffizi Gallery.* The medal, in gilded stucco, is the posthumous one struck in honor of Cosimo the Elder when he was declared the "Father of the

Fatherland" after his death in 1464. Willed to the Uffizi in 1666 by Cardinal Carlo de' Medici, the panel was listed as anonymous in the early inventories. In 1825, it bore the name of Filippino Lippi, and later, Andrea del Castagno until late in the nineteenth century when it was attributed to Botticelli by Morelli, Frizzoni and Ulmann. Everyone accepts the attribution except Bode, who thinks it is inferior.

The sitter has been identified at various times as one or another member of the Medici family, but the chronology of the painting refutes the identification. Some critics have identified the sitter as the artist who executed the medal—Michelozzo, Niccolò Fiorentino, or Cristoforo Geremia.

While the quality of the painting advises against dating it early in the painter's career, the persistence of Pollaiuolo-like elements and the presence of definite analogies with the *St Sebastian* in Berlin compel us to date it around 1473–74.

Plate 48a

PORTRAIT OF LORENZO THE MAGNIFICENT. *Panel, 55 × 37. Formerly in Paris, Lazzaroni Collection.* The portrait came from the Isolani family collection (Castelvecchio, near Bologna), from which the *Portrait of Giuliano de' Medici*, now in the Crespi Collection (plate 48b) was later acquired. Generally neglected by critics, the portrait is considered autograph by Yashiro (who mistakes the sitter as Giuliano), Van Marle and Mesnil. Probably datable around 1475 (see comment on next plate).

Plate 48b

PORTRAIT OF GIULIANO DE' MEDICI. *Panel, 54.5 × 36.5. Milan,* *Crespi Collection.* Once in the Isolani family collection along with the *Portrait of Lorenzo the Magnificent* (see plate 48a), it went from the Kahn Collection in New York to the Thyssen Collection in Lugano and finally in 1956 to the Crespi Collection. It was published for the first time as a Botticelli in *The Times* (April 1, 1914), by Fry (*The Burlington Magazine*) and in *Art in America* (April 1914); it is unquestionably original. While the pendant portrait exists only in the original, there are three other versions of the *Portrait of Giuliano de' Medici*—in Bergamo, Berlin and Washington, D.C.—and critics are in sharp disagreement about which are original and which are workshop copies. Morelli, Ulmann and Berenson favor the Bergamo version as Botticelli's work. Horne attributes it to "Sandro's friend." Bode, Van Marle and Yashiro agree on the Berlin version as autograph, although Yashiro considers it the best and a copy. Berenson thinks it is a copy partially done by Botticelli. The Milan portrait is considered authentic by both A. and L. Venturi, Valentiner, Gamba, Mesnil and Berenson himself, who considered it equal to the Bergamo version. The Washington *Portrait* is seconded by Bettini, Suida and Shapley in the National Gallery's catalog (*Paintings and Sculptures Acquired from the Kress Foundation,* 1956), where Berenson expressed a supporting opinion. Without comparing the paintings directly, it is difficult to make a final judgment. Bettini's persuasive hypothesis that the Washington version, painted when Giuliano was alive, probably on the occasion of the tourney in 1475, is the archetype for the other three posthumous portraits meets with two objections: the turtle-dove

47

(as Friedman points out in the National Gallery catalog) and the open door were funereal symbols since classic times. Thus this version is probably posthumous. The second objection is the anomaly of the elongated bust, despite the high quality of the painting, while the other versions have much shorter busts. The difference would seem to indicate that the Washington *Portrait* is a copy. The Milan version is equally fine. It is turned in the opposite direction from the others, and so could easily be the pendant to the *Portrait of Lorenzo* (plate 48a). We contend that Botticelli painted this first (note the more open eyes) while Giuliano was alive, around 1475. The other three versions may have been painted by Botticelli and his workshop, as memorials for friends of the Medici immediately after Giuliano's assassination in 1478.

Color Plate IV

PORTRAIT OF A YOUNG WOMAN.

Plate 49a

PORTRAIT OF GIULIANO DE' MEDICI. *Panel, 54 × 36. Bergamo, Accademia Carrara.* From the Morelli Collection. A reverse copy, partly autograph, of the version illustrated in plate 48b.

Plate 49b

PORTRAIT OF GIULIANO DE' MEDICI. *Panel, 54 × 36. Berlin, Staaliche Museen.* From the Strozzi Palace in Florence, noted by Caval-caselle as Botticelli's work in 1864. Reverse copy, partially autograph, of the version in plate 48b.

Plate 50

PORTRAIT OF GIULIANO DE' MEDICI. *Panel, 76 × 52.6. Washington, D.C., National Gallery, Kress Collection.* The Kress Collection acquired it from a private Italian collection in 1949. Bettini claimed it as the archetypal version in 1942. Reverse version, enlarged and partially autograph, of the painting in plate 48b.

Plate 51

PORTRAIT OF A YOUNG WOMAN. *Panel, 61 × 40. Pitto Palace Gallery.* Traditionally identified as one of the "two heads of women in profile, very lovely, one of whom is the beloved of Giuliano de' Medici" cited by Vasari in 1568 "in the possession of Duke Cosimo." Thus the old inventories called the sitter Simonetta Vespucci. But the sitter and painter are both subject to controversy. Since we have no authentic portraits of Simonetta, or a description of her, it is impossible to ascertain if the sitter is Simonetta, Giuliano's mistress, and wife of the Genoese Marco Vespucci. Horne suggested Fioretta Gorini, who became Giuliano's mistress after Simonetta died, and mother of Giulio de' Medici (later Pope Clement VII). But all the proposals are merely hypothetical. As for the painter, there are a number of critics who do not think it is Botticelli's work. On the other hand, Ulmann, Bode, Schmarsow, A. Venturi, L. Venturi, Mesnil and Bettini think it is and date the painting from 1478 (Gamba) to as late as 1490 (Bode, A. Venturi). As far as I can see, the style and quality of the painting are unquestionably in Botticelli's favor. The Pollaiuolo reminiscences would date it around 1475. Indeed there is no reason to doubt Vasari that here we do see the lovely Simonetta.

Plate 52

ADORATION OF THE MAGI. *Panel, 111 × 134. Florence, Uffizi Gallery.*

Albertini is the first to mention the panel in his *Memoriale* (1510) as "... the Magi, between the doors [of Santa Maria Novella], by Sandro Botticelli." The *Libro di Antonio Billi* (Petrei Codex, 1516–30) cites "a panel in Santa Maria Novella by the middle door," painted by Sandro. The *Anonimo Gaddiano* is more precise: "... and in S. Maria Novella he painted a small altar panel near the center door of the *magi* who are painted naturalistically." Vasari goes so far as to identify the first King as a portrait of Cosimo the Elder and the second King as that of Giuliano de' Medici. In the second edition of his *Lives* he identifies the third King as Giovanni, Cosimo's son. Mesnil published some documents in 1903 showing that the panel was painted for Giovanni Lami's altar at the right of the main door. Other patrons of the altar followed; the Fedini family and then Fabio Mandragoni, a Spanish merchant, who had it remodeled after Vasari's design. Botticelli's painting was removed toward the end of the sixteenth century, and reappeared in 1796 in the Medici Villa at Poggio Imperiale. It was acquired by the Uffizi as a Ghirlandaio, and the attribution remained until 1845, when Carlo Pini recognized it as a Botticelli. Scholars have tried to ascertain the identity of the various personages. Vasari was probably right as to the first and third Kings, but the second King is obviously not Giuliano. Ulmann convincingly argues that Baldassare is the portrait of Piero the Gouty (died 1469), the young man standing behind him is Giuliano, the young man in the extreme right foreground is a self-portrait of the artist, the young man with the plumed hat is Lorenzo Tornabuoni, the old man turned

three-quarters near the wall on the right is Filippo Strozzi and the young man on the left, with a sword, is Lorenzo the Magnificent (the man embracing him may be Poliziano). Not all critics agree with this identification. In any case, the portraits of Cosimo, Piero the Gouty and Giovanni as the three Kings, and Giuliano and Lorenzo (right and left respectively) are fairly certain. Less certain is the self-portrait.

The dating is problematic. Some critics relate it to the Pazzi conspiracy in 1478 (the portraits would thus be commemorative); others judge from the age of the personages and date the painting earlier. But these are quite hypothetical arguments. We consider that the painting appears to be earlier than the *Primavera* with its musical resolution of line and space, that the Pollaiuolo qualities are here modified, while the intarsias executed in 1476 after Botticelli's designs on several doors of the Ducal Palace in Urbino (see Attributed Paintings, plates 146–151) show that artist's style in this period was still strongly influenced by Pollaiuolo. We conclude that the probable date for this *Adoration* was about 1476–77.

Plate 53

ADORATION OF THE MAGI. Detail: the Virgin and Child, with St Joseph and Melchior (Cosimo the Elder?).

Plate 54

ADORATION OF THE MAGI. Detail: group on the left, including portrait of Lorenzo the Magnificent (first figure at the left).

Plate 55

ADORATION OF THE MAGI. Detail: group on the right with portraits of Giovanni de' Medici (first figure at

49

the left), of Giuliano de' Medici (dark young man near the bush) and the probable self-portrait of the artist (last figure on the right; cf. plate 57).

Plate 56

ADORATION OF THE MAGI. Detail: St Joseph.

Plate 57

ADORATION OF THE MAGI. Detail: Botticelli's probable self-portrait.

Plate 58

THREE ANGELS. *Drawing, 10 × 23.5. Florence, Uffizi Gallery*. Pen and white lead on rose paper. Berenson, Giglioli, Bode, Ede, Yashiro, Popham, Van Marle, Gamba, and Bettini all agree the drawing is by Botticelli. Considered as a late work by some, it really should be dated closer to the *Primavera*.

Plate 59

THE NATIVITY. *Fresco, about 200 × 300. Florence, Church of Santa Maria Novella.* Once known as a work of the "Florentine School of the fifteenth century," or sometimes attributed to Filippo Lippi, the fresco was recognized as a Botticelli by Berenson and Gamba (1932), who submits that it may have been part of the decoration of the Lami Chapel. In that case, it would be contemporary with the *Adoration of the Magi* (see comment on plate 52).

The fresco is now located in a pointed lunette on the inside of the church, over the central door, but originally it was semicircular and was so it appears "made over" for the new location. The work is probably Botticelli's, because it reveals a number of his characteristics and because, deriving its composition from Lippi's *Nativity* in Spoleto, it has that softness and formal freedom which mark the *Adoration* in the Uffizi. Datable around 1476–77.

Plate 60

PORTRAIT OF A YOUTH. *Panel, 51 × 36. Washington, D.C., National Gallery.* Acquired by the Mellon Collection (and thus going to the National Gallery) from the Leichtenstein Gallery through the Stout Collection of Chicago. Although a number of critics have ascribed the *Portrait* to Botticelli (including Schmarsow, Van Marle, L. Venturi and Mesnil), most recent criticism has tended to ascribe it to Filippino. A relationship is pointed out between this panel and a figure Vasari mentions in Filippino's frescoes in the Carmine. But the sustained vigor of the line assuredly indicates a work by Botticelli, painted a little earlier than the *Primavera*. I have reconfirmed it as autograph (1957). Dates range from 1470 (Kroeber) to as late as 1480 (L. Venturi and Mesnil).

Plate 61

PORTRAIT OF A MAN. *Panel, 51.5 × 35. Formerly in Naples, Museo Filangieri.* Destroyed during the war. It came from the Filangieri Castle in Sapio. Once attributed to Ghirlandaio, it was recognized as Botticelli's work by Frizzoni in 1889. Berenson attributed it to "Sandro's friend," and Venturi rejected it as an imitation. The close affinities between this *Portrait* and the portraits in the *Adoration of the Magi* (plate 52), along with an opening toward more synthetic plastic structure, lead me to date this around 1476–77.

LOCATION OF PAINTINGS

AJACCIO
  MUSÉE FESCH
  Madonna and Child with Angel
  (plate 2).

ALTENBURG
              (GERMANY)
  LINDENAU MUSEUM
  Portrait of a Woman as St Catherine
  (plate 37).

BARCELONA
  CAMBÓ COLLECTION
  *Story of Nastagio degli Onesti, First
  Episode* (plate 141; attribution)
  *Story of Nastagio degli Onesti, Second
  Episode* (plate 142; attribution).
  *Story of Nastagio degli Onesti, Third
  Episode* (plate 143; attribution).

BERGAMO
  ACCADEMIA CARRARA
  Portrait of Giuliano de' Medici
  (plate 49a).

BERLIN
  STAATLICHE MUSEEN
  St Sebastian (plate 45).
  Portrait of Giuliano de' Medici
  (plate 49b).
  Raczinsky Tondo (plate 63).
  Portrait of a Young Man (plate 134a;
  attribution).

BESANÇON
  MUSÉE DES BEAUX-ARTS
  Portrait of a Boy (plate 132; attri-
  bution).

BOSTON
  ISABELLA STEWART GARDNER
  MUSEUM
  Madonna of the Eucharist (plate 35).

CHANTILLY
  MUSÉE CONDÉ
  Pomona (plate 140; attribution).

CHARLBURY
              (ENGLAND)
  WATNEY COLLECTION
  *Story of Nastagio degli Onesti, Fourth
  Episode* (plate 144; attribution).

CHERBOURG
  MUSÉE DE PEINTURE
  Deposition (see p. 80, "Attributed
  Paintings").

CHICAGO
  EPSTEIN COLLECTION
  Madonna and Child with a Boy (plate
  128; attribution).

DETROIT
  INSTITUTE OF ARTS
  Resurrected Christ (plate 106).

EDINBURGH
  NATIONAL GALLERY OF SCOT-
  LAND
  Portrait of a Young Man (see p. 81,
  "Attributed Paintings").

FLORENCE
  ACCADEMIA
  *Madonna and Child with St John the
  Baptist* (plates 6–7).
  Madonna of the Sea (plate 62).

51

VICTORIA AND ALBERT MUSEUM
Portrait of Esmeralda Bandinelli (?) (plate 36).

MANHASSET (NEW YORK)

BRADY COLLECTION
Madonna and Child with Angels (plate 126; attribution).

MARSEILLES

MUSÉE DES BEAUX-ARTS
Madonna and Child (see p. 81, "Attributed Paintings").

MILAN

CRESPI COLLECTION
Portrait of Giuliano de' Medici (plate 48b).

NAPLES

MUSEO FILANGIERI
Portrait of a Young Man (plate 133b; attribution).

NATIONAL GALLERIES OF CAPODIMONTE
Madonna and Child with Angels (plate 12b).

NEW YORK

BLUMENTHAL COLLECTION
Madonna and Child, fragment (see p. 80, "Attributed Paintings").

DUVEEN COLLECTION
Madonna and Child with Youth (plate 10).

METROPOLITAN MUSEUM OF ART
Havemayer Madonna (plate 125; attribution).
Portrait of a Young Man (plate 133a; attribution).

PARIS

LOUVRE
Guidi Madonna (plate 4).
Madonna and Child (plate 5).
Madonna and Child with St John (plates 8–9).
Madonna and Child with Angels (plate 14).
Lorenzo Tornabuoni [?] *and the Graces* (plates 116, 118–120).
A Lady and four Allegorical Figures (plates 117, 121–124).
Madonna and Child with Angels (plate 139; attribution).
Portrait of a Young Man (plate 145; attribution).

PHILADELPHIA

JOHN G. JOHNSON ART COLLECTION
Christ Teaching (plate 26).
Feast in the House of Simon (plate 27).
"Noli me tangere" (plate 28).
Last Moments of Mary Magdalen (plate 29).
Portrait of a Young Man (plate 138; attribution).

PIACENZA

MUSEO CIVICO
Madonna and Child with St John the Baptist (plate 83).

RENNES (FRANCE)

MUSÉE DES BEAUX-ARTS
Head of an Angel (drawing, plate 136).

SANTA MONICA (CALIFORNIA)

BARBARA HUTTON COLLECTION
Portrait of a Young Man (plate 18).

STOCKHOLM

ROYAL COLLECTION
Portrait of a Young Man (see pp. 81–82, "Attributed Paintings").

MUSÉE DES BEAUX-ARTS
Madonna and Child with Angels
(plate 13a).

URBINO
DUCAL PALACE
*Intarsias of the Door of the Sala degli
Angeli* (plates 146–151; attribution).

VATICAN CITY
SISTINE CHAPEL
Pope St Evaristus (plate 84a).
Pope St Cornelius (plate 84b).
Pope St Sixtus (plate 85a).
Pope St Marcellinus (plate 85b).
Pope St Stephen (plate 86a).
Pope St Soter (plate 86b).
Pope St Lucius (plate 86c).
Scenes from the Life of Moses (plates
87–91).
Temptation of Christ (plates 92–99).
Punishment of Korah (plates 100–
105).

WASHINGTON, D.C.
NATIONAL GALLERY OF ART
Madonna and Child (plate 11).

Portrait of Giuliano de' Medici
(plate 50).
Portrait of a Youth (plate 60).
Adoration of the Magi (plates 108–
111).

ZÜRICH
ALEGG STOCKAR COLLECTION
St Thomas Aquinas (plate 82).

LOCATION UNKNOWN
Portrait of a Medici, formerly in
Florence, Corsini Gallery (plate
46).
Portrait of Lorenzo the Magnificent,
formerly in Paris, Lazzaroni Collection (plate 48a).
Madonna Enthroned, formerly in
Wantage, England, Lloyd Collection (plate 129; attribution).
Portrait of a Youth, formerly in
Zürich, Abels Collection (plate
134b; attribution).
*Madonna and Child with St John the
Baptist*, formerly in Munich,
Nemès Collection (see pp. 80–81,
"Attributed Paintings").

DESTROYED
Portrait of a Man, formerly in
Naples, Museo Filangieri (plate
61).

REPRODUCTIONS

ACKNOWLEDGMENT FOR
PLATES

B. Anderson, Rome: plates 1, 6, 11, 12b, 16, 19, 20, 43, 47, 49a, 51, 53–55, 61, 64–65, 66, 72–73, 75, 83–92, 94–99, 102–105, 107, 133b, 146–148, 150b. *Alinari, Florence:* 3, 7–9, 14–15, 17, 21, 46, 57, 59, 68–69, 71, 74, 93, 100–101, 116–124, 132, 139, 145. *Gabinetto Fotografico della Sovrintendenza alle Gallerie, Florence:* 22–25, 30, 44, 52, 58, 62, 78, 80–81b, 113–115, 127, 135. *Brogi, Florence:* 67, 70, 76, 77, 79. *Duveen Brothers, New York:* 10, 18. *National Gallery, London:* 12a, 13b, 32–33, 34, 38–42, 137. *Johnson Collection, Philadelphia:* 26–29, 138. *Walter Steinkopf, Berlin-Dahlem:* 45, 49b, 63. *National Gallery of Art, Washington, D.C.:* 50, 60, 108–111. *A. y. R. Mas, Barcelona:* 141–143. *Bulloz, Paris:* 2. *Archives Photographiques des Monuments Historiques de France, Paris:* 4. *Jean-Pierre Sudre, Paris:* 5. *George Philip Sauter, Glens Falls, New York:* 31. *Gardner Museum, Boston:* 35. *Victoria and Albert Museum, London:* 36. *Kunsthistorisches Institut, Leipzig:* 37. *A. Reali, Florence:* 56. *Institute of Art, Detroit:* 106. *British Museum, London:* 112. *Art Institute, Chicago:* 128. *Metropolitan Museum of Art, New York:* 133a. *Bildarchiv Foto, Marburg:* 134a. *Musée des Beaux-Arts, Rennes:* 136. The other illustrations are taken from the author's own files.
Material for all color plates was supplied by Scala, Florence.

DISCOVERY OF THE MURDER OF HOLOFERNES
Florence, Uffizi Gallery
(*detail of plate 43*)

Plate 1. MADONNA AND CHILD Florence, Museo dell'Ospedale degli Innocenti

Plate 2. MADONNA AND CHILD WITH ANGEL Ajaccio, Musée Fesch

Plate 3. MADONNA OF THE LOGGIA Florence, Uffizi Gallery

Plate 4. GUIDI MADONNA Paris, Louvre

Plate 5. MADONNA AND CHILD Paris, Louvre

Plate 6. MADONNA AND CHILD WITH ST JOHN THE BAPTIST Florence,
Accademia

Plate 7. *Detail of plate 6*

Plate 8. MADONNA AND CHILD WITH ST JOHN Paris, Louvre

Plate 9. *Detail of plate 8*

Plate 10. MADONNA AND CHILD WITH YOUTH New York, Duveen
Collection

Plate 11. MADONNA AND CHILD Washington, D.C., National Gallery

Plate 12. MADONNA AND CHILD London, National Gallery
MADONNA AND CHILD WITH ANGELS Naples, Capodimonte

Plate 13. MADONNA AND CHILD WITH ANGELS Strasbourg, Musée des Beaux-Arts and London, National Gallery

Plate 14. MADONNA AND CHILD WITH ANGELS Paris, Louvre

Plate 15. MADONNA IN GLORY WITH SERAPHIM Florence, Uffizi
Gallery

Plate 16. MADONNA OF THE ROSE ARBOR Florence, Uffizi Gallery

JUDITH WITH THE HEAD OF HOLOFERNES
Florence, Uffizi Gallery

Plate 17. *Detail of plate 16*

Plate 18. PORTRAIT OF A YOUNG MAN Santa Monica, California,
Barbara Hutton Collection

Plate 19. PORTRAIT OF A YOUTH Florence, Pitti Palace

Plate 20. FORTITUDE Florence, Uffizi Gallery

Plate 21. *Detail of plate 20*

Plate 22. ALTARPIECE OF THE CONVERTITE (?) Florence, Uffizi
Gallery

Plate 23. *Detail of plate 22*

Plate 24. *Detail of plate 22*

Plate 25. *Detail of plate 22*

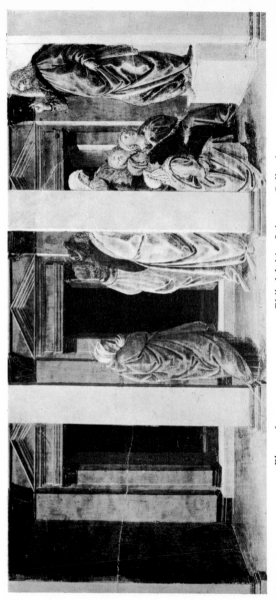

Plate 26. CHRIST TEACHING Philadelphia, Johnson Collection

Plate 27. FEAST IN THE HOUSE OF SIMON Philadelphia, Johnson
Collection

Plate 28. "NOLI ME TANGERE" Philadelphia, Johnson Collection

Plate 29. LAST MOMENTS OF MARY MAGDALEN Philadelphia,
Johnson Collection

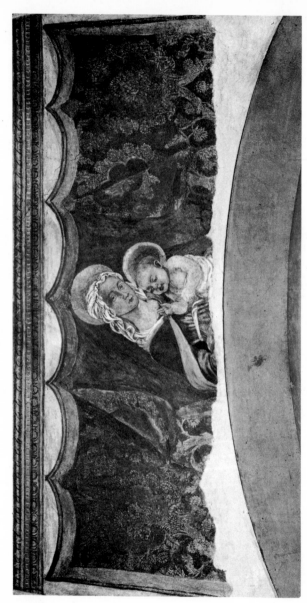

Plate 30. MADONNA AND CHILD Florence, Church of the Annunziata

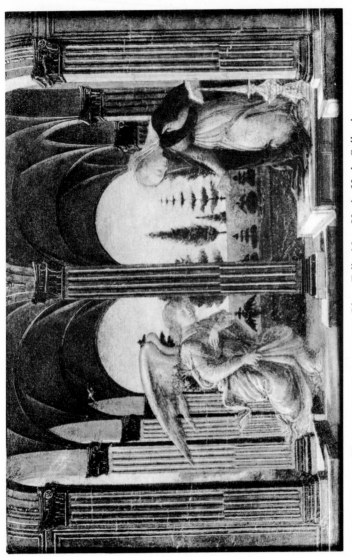

Plate 31. ANNUNCIATION Glens Falls, New York, Hyde Collection

Plates 32–33. ADORATION OF TH

AGI London, National Gallery

Plate 34. *Detail of plates 32–33*

Plate 35. MADONNA OF THE EUCHARIST Boston, Isabella Gardner
Museum

Plate 36. PORTRAIT OF ESMERALDA BANDINELLI (?) London,
Victoria and Albert Museum

Plate 37. PORTRAIT OF A WOMAN AS ST CATHERINE Altenburg,
Lindenau Museum

Plate 38. TONDO: THE ADORATION OF THE MAGI London,
National Gallery

Plate 39. *Detail of plate 38*

Plate 40. Detail of plate 38

PORTRAIT OF A MAN WITH A MEDAL
Florence, Uffizi Gallery

Plate 41. *Detail of plate 38*

Plate 42. *Detail of plate 38*

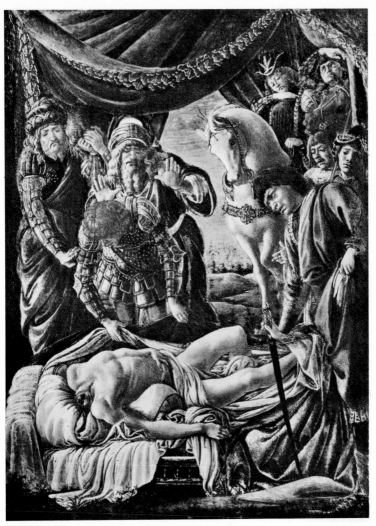

Plate 43. DISCOVERY OF THE MURDER OF HOLOFERNES Florence,
Uffizi Gallery

Plate 44. JUDITH WITH THE HEAD OF HOLOFERNES Florence,
Uffizi Gallery

Plate 45. ST SEBASTIAN Berlin, Staatliche Museen

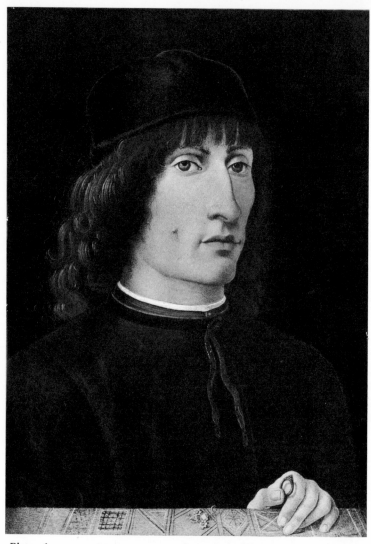

Plate 46. PORTRAIT OF A MEDICI formerly in Florence, Corsini Gallery

Plate 47. PORTRAIT OF A MAN WITH A MEDAL Florence, Uffizi Gallery

Plate 48. PORTRAIT OF LORENZO THE MAGNIFICENT formerly in
Paris, Lazzaroni Collection

PORTRAIT OF GIULIANO DE' MEDICI Milan, Crespi Collection

PORTRAIT OF A YOUNG WOMAN
Florence, Uffizi Gallery

Plate 49. PORTRAIT OF GIULIANO DE' MEDICI Bergamo, Accademia
Carrara and Berlin, Staatliche Museen

Plate 50. PORTRAIT OF GIULIANO DE' MEDICI Washington, D.C.,
National Gallery

Plate 51. PORTRAIT OF A YOUNG WOMAN Florence, Pitti Palace

Plate 52. ADORATION OF THE MAGI Florence, Uffizi Gallery

Plate 53. *Detail of plate 52*

Plate 54. *Detail of plate 52*

Plate 55. *Detail of plate 52*

Plate 56. *Detail of plate 52*

Plate 57. *Detail of plate 52*

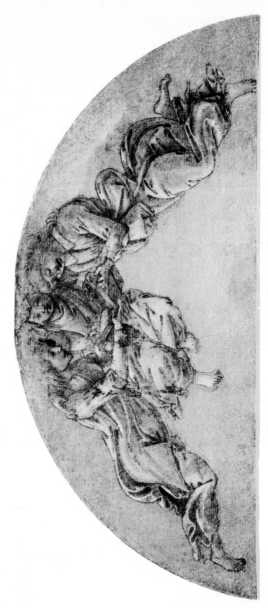

Plate 58. THREE ANGELS Florence, Uffizi Gallery

Plate 59. THE NATIVITY Florence, Church of Santa Maria Novella

Plate 60. PORTRAIT OF A YOUNG MAN Washington, D.C., National
Gallery

Plate 61. PORTRAIT OF A MAN formerly in Naples, Museo Filangieri

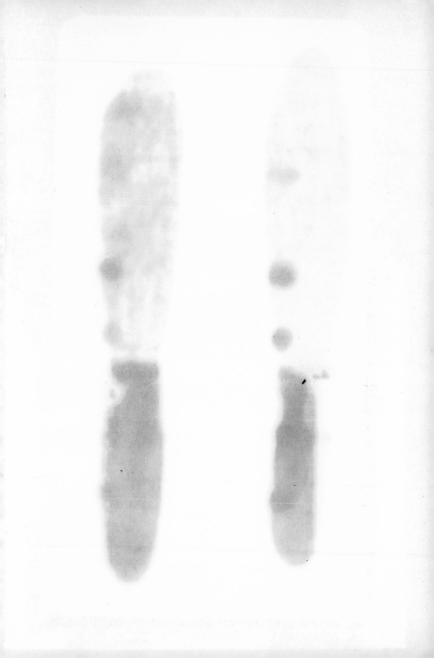

DATE DUE
